I0434820

With Love, From Angel

Copyright © 2014 by Angel Miller
All rights reserved under
International and Pan-American
Copyright Conventions.

Library of Congress Cataloging-In-Publication
Data

Miller, Angel or Angel the Alien
    With Love, From Angel /Angel Miller
    Trixie Pixie Publications
    I. ADHD-patient stories II Autism

http://diaryofanalien1.blogspot.com

This book is dedicated to...

TRISH SAMMER JOHNSTON because of all she did to make my autism evaluation possible

and her daughter MEGAN, a fellow Aspie girl and budding blogger...

and to WILLIAM and his mother MARY for their friendship and support

and to ALL my blog readers, because I wrote this for you!

Table Of Contents

Disclaimer

Thank you for reading this book!

I am: – A person with autism and ADHD
– A person with a lot of experience working with children who have special needs.
– A person with a special education teaching degree.

I am not: – A doctor
– An autism or ADHD expert
– A representative of the thoughts and opinions of ALL people with ADHD or autism.

The pages you are about to read include my thoughts, opinions, and things I have learned. This is, in a way, a personal letter from me to you.

I write mostly about autism and ADHD. But the material here could be applied to all types of neurodiversity... mental illness, learning disabilities, Traumatic Brain Injury, Tourette Syndrome, cognitive disabilities, etc.

My main point is that _everyone_ is different, and _everyone_ deserves respect and love.

Hi From Angel!

Who am I? I am an alien!

You may think that I'm being silly.

You may say that you don't believe in aliens. But the Merriam-Webster Dictionary's definition of the word "alien" includes, "Differing in nature or character typically to the point of incompatibility." Other definitions include, "Dissimilar, inconsistent, or opposed, as in nature," "A person who is not included in a group," and "an outsider." These all describe me pretty well!

I've been diagnosed with a plethora of disorders, including Aspergers and ADHD, each of which explains some but not all aspects of me and my life.

I was 7 years old when I began to suspect I was an alien. I expected the people from my home planet to come collect me at any time. This alternately excited me, and made me sad. I was excited at the idea of someday having a place to belong, but I also knew I'd miss Earth.

It was very confusing!

I used to love to put out my arms and spin around and around, until lights and colors swirled around me. I thought I might reach some sort of meditative state that would allow me to contact my alien family.

As far as I know it never worked. Eventually I gave up... although I still enjoy spinning around! And I still feel like an alien!

Maybe I really am from a different planet, where all of the inhabitants are like me. But until that planet is discovered, I have to learn to survive here on Earth.

What I Wish People Knew About...
AUTISM!

This is a list I've written, drawing on my own experiences having Aspergers* working with children with autism spectrum disorders, and talking with others who have autism spectrum disorders. However, autism is different for everyone. Not all people with autism will experience everything on this list in the same ways that I do.

① We have feelings! I'm pretty sure this one is actually true of all people, with or without autism.

There is a myth that people with autism don't feel emotions the way other people do. This probably dates back to the Refrigerator Mother theory of the 1940's and 50's. When autism was first identified, it was believed that it was caused by mothers who were so cold and unemotional with their children, that the children never developed emotions such as joy or love, and never developed a connection to the rest of the world. (There actually is a disorder caused by circumstances similar to that BUT it is not autism... and if your kids have not been confined to an orphanage crib for most of their lives, or been severely abused or neglected, they probably DON'T have that.)

In 2012, a man walked into a school and began shooting teachers and children, before eventually taking

④

his own life. Afterwards, it came out in the media that the man had once been diagnosed with Aspergers Syndrome. This helped to perpetuate the idea that people with autism were disturbed, unfeeling, and potentially dangerous.

The truth is, we _do_ have emotions. But some of us have trouble recognizing and expressing our emotions. Kids with autism often have trouble learning things that are not concrete... things that can't be seen, heard, and touched. So a child may feel sad, but not understand what it is, why he feels it, or how to express it.

Here is one of my infamous "imagine this" examples. Imagine you have two 6-year-old children... one with autism, one without. Imagine their pet fish dies. The child without autism (let's call him Bobby) may react in the ways you might expect from a child. He may cry, need lots of hugs and reassurance, and ask to have a funeral for his fish. The other child (let's call him Tommy) may not cry at all. He may appear completely unbothered! He may express interest in looking at the fish's body, and be very curious in a scientific way. This may seem creepy to a parent. You might think, "Tommy had no attachment to the fish. Tommy doesn't care if the fish lived or died."

In reality, Tommy may very well feel sadness over the loss of his pet fish. But he may not

⑤

recognize his feeling as "sad," or understand why he is feeling it. Instead of expressing his sadness by crying, he may react by being irritable, being resistant to any other interruptions in his routine, avoiding being reminded of the fish, or trying to understand the idea of death.

I once knew a boy whose pet fish did die. He reacted by refusing to acknowleadge that the fish was not there! He would talk to the fish, while looking at the spot where the fish bowl used to be, and even pretend to feed the fish. He'd get upset if anyone tried to remind him that his fish had died!

By the way, that is one of the examples that DOESN't apply to me. I've always been OVERLY emotionally reactive... especially when it comes to animals!

② We can love others. This is related to #1, but I thought it deserved its own section.

Parents of children with autism used to be told that their children would be incapable of loving them. I hope that isn't true anymore! We do feel love for our family members, friends, pets, etc.

Just like other emotions, expressing love doesn't always come naturally to people with autism. For instance, a lot of people like to express love with kisses and hugs. If your child with autism doesn't want to hug you or get a bedtime kiss from you, it isn't because he doesn't feel love

⑥

for you. It may mean that the feeling of being hugged or kissed is unpleasant for them. The closeness, the texture and scent of your clothing, and the pressure of a hug or wetness of a kiss, may be too much for him. Some parents compromise by asking their child for a side hug or one-armed hug. (On the other hand, some people love the squeezing pressure of a bear hug!)

People with autism can also have trouble acting loving towards people they honestly don't feel love for. For example, if you ask your child to hug and kiss your elderly aunt, whom he is meeting for the first time, he might balk. He may not even want to say "I love you" to the person. After all, how can he love someone he just met?

But let me reassure you that, yes, your children do love you. You might just have to get to know the ways that they express it.

♥ ♥ ♥ ♥ ♥ ♥

③ <u>We can feel empathy</u>. This is also related to the first two. People with autism may have difficulty recognizing signs that someone is feeling emotions. A lot of adults I've known have told me that they learned as children to recognize the obvious

⑦

signs... such as a person who is frowning or crying is sad, while a person who is smiling is happy. But subtle differences... such as a person who is frowning because he is either sad, angry, or scared... can be harder. So can situations where people cover up their emotions such as a person who smiles and says they are "fine" when they are actually angry.

So, a person who accepts' others emotions at "face value" might be seen as lacking empathy. Really, they just need more concrete clues as to what another person is feeling.

Also, a person who understands that someone is feeling an emotion might not be sure how to react. Or they may not be able to react in the expected ways.

I went through this when a friend of mine was going through a divorce. I knew she was feeling sad and angry. I wanted to help her, but I didn't know how to comfort her. I tried to act extra cheerful around her, and I helped her around the house. But to my friend, it seemed as though I didn't care what she was going through. Another friend of hers spent a lot of time hugging her and talking comfortingly to her, and my friend percieved that person as really caring about her.

⑧

Some people with autism say that they are actually extremely sensitive to others' feelings. They may actually feel what the other person is feeling, to the point of discomfort. Not only may they not be sure how to react, but they may feel so overwhelmed by the feeling that they "shut down" and tune out.

④ <u>We want to have friends.</u> Another old myth is that people with autism do not enjoy friends, and do not get lonely. This may be true for some people, both with and without autism. We all know people who are a little grumpy around other people and need their "alone time."

But most of us do want to have friends, and do feel lonely. I definitely do need time alone, but I also long to have friends. It is hard for me to make friends as an adult, just as it was when I was a kid, because my interests and the things I enjoy doing are still different from a lot of the other people I know.

Many adult women my age like going shopping in high-end stores, going to wine tastings or cocktail parties, getting together to watch a sport, or going bar hopping. A lot of these activities are centered around small talk or "chit chat." I prefer activities like doing arts and crafts, going river tubing, or going to Six Flags. I am just not good at sitting around and making

⑨

light conversation about trivial topics!

Another problem is that people with autism might not know how to approach people to make friends. When I was a little kid, I had a formulaic approach that served me pretty well. I'd walk up to a kid and ask them three questions: "What's your name?" "How old are you?" and "Want to play?" This worked well when I was so young that most of my friendships were 100% play based. But after I was about 9 or 10, it didn't work anymore... it actually seemed to have the opposite effect, causing other kids to give me strange looks and walk away.

I also have trouble knowing the difference between a "friend" and an ~~acquaintance~~ "acquaintance." When I was a kid, I thought anyone who was somewhat friendly to me wanted to be my friend. Even as an adult, I still have this problem. If someone is nice to me, I think they are my new best friend! It is hard for me to accept that, just because a neighbor talks to me for ten minutes, that doesn't mean they will ever actually want to hang out with me.

You may say, "But Angel, if you are writing about it, then you DO understand it!" My answer to that is, although I understand it because I've been taught it, I still rarely recognize it when it happens. Once not long ago, a person who worked in the same building as me showed me some friendliness. She told me about her dog, to be specific. We would say "hi" to each other whenever we saw each other. I would ask her about her dog, who was sick, and she would give me updates.

On my last day of working there, I gave her my contact info, thinking we could "hang out." But she never e-mailed me. Still thinking our conversations at work had been meaningful, I took it a step further, found her on Facebook, and sent her a private message and a friend request. She rejected me.

I thought we were friends, but really she was just being polite to me because we were at work. Did I understand, at the time, that sometimes people are friendly just to be polite? Yes. Did I recognize that when it happened? No. And it still stings! ☹

⑤ We kinda need to "stim." I hate the word "stim", but I don't really know another word for it. Usually stimming is a repetetive motion that someone frequently does. For instance, I rock back and forth (which is a stereotypical stim, although I have not met many other people who do it, outside of fictional autistic characters), flap my fingers, hum, and other things. When I was a kid I used to flap my arms at my sides. I also used to twirl my hair, until one day I twirled it so much that a huge knotted chunk came right out of my head. It frightened me so much that I screamed, and my mom told me never to twirl my hair again. I still twirl my hair, but just not enough

⑪

to leave bald spots!

Jumping up and down, grunting, or clapping, are more examples of stims. I know a boy who could spin around in circles for hours, if left uninterrupted.

When we stim, we are trying to calm and regulate ourselves. I'm not sure how that works, but it does. When I rock back and forth, it kind of feels like gravity is pushing against me, and it helps me feel calm and less anxious. Sometimes I also rock just because I'm bored and need to move.

I hear a lot of teachers scolding kids for stimming. Teachers will hate me for saying this, because many people who work with those with autism want to teach them to look "normal" and fit in with others, and stimming brings attention to our differences.

But telling us not to stim can be like telling someone not to scratch an itch or not to swallow. You just feel like you need to do it, and if you concentrate on not doing it, you start feeling uncomfortable and anxious.

I love when schools have a "motor room" or "sensory room" where kids can go. They usually have things like indoor swings, exercise trampolines, mats and tunnels for crawling on things for climbing, places to roll, etc. I think kids should be able to get their "stimmies" out, especially right before a time when they're going to be expected to sit still and concentrate. "Deep pressure" activities like swinging, jumping and climbing help to calm and center people with autism, and can reduce their need to stim.

If your child's stimming attracts a lot of negative attention, you can try to teach him to do something less obvious or while he's out in public. Squeezing a stress ball, putting on chapstick, chewing gum or hard candy, wiggling your feet, or crossing your arms to give yourself a squeeze, can help. But once they get into the privacy of their own home, they should be allowed to relax and let go.

⑥ <u>Push us to improve</u>... without <u>pushing too hard</u>.
My parents didn't know, when I was a child, that I had Aspergers or ADHD. They just thought I was weird, and they wanted me to be normal. My mom often pushed me to be more like the other kids. She would tell me that if I did, or didn't do, certain things, others would think I was weird and they wouldn't like me.

When I was in high school, a psychologist told my mom that I would never be able to drive a can, go to college, get a job or live on my own. My mom was upset, but then she became determined to make sure I did do all of those things. The problem was that she pushed me so hard, and put in place such dire consequences for not doing these things, that I ended up doing them all before I was ready... and failing miserably.

My advice is, know your kid. Don't know him in comparison to other kids his age, or in comparison to his older siblings and cousins and neighbors. Know him for himself, your child. Let your specific child be the guide for what he is or isn't ready to do. If you really, really want him to be on the soccer team, but he adamantly tells you he hates soccer, listen to him. Think about why you want him to be in soccer. Is it so he can get extra physical activity? Maybe he'd be interested in another sport... maybe a more individualized one like running or swimming. If you were hoping he'd learn about teamwork, try to find another team activity. I've heard of a really cool activity for kids with autism, where they work together to make stop-motion movies out of Legos. If your goal was for him to make friends, try Boy Scouts, Campfire USA, or a group based on one of his interests.

(14)

If you were hoping he'd play soccer because many of your friends are "soccer moms" and you want to join them... I hate to tell you, but you may have to give up on that.

This can be even harder as your kid gets older. He's going to want to be more independent, but he may also need help in some areas. Recognize that it isn't an all or nothing situation. It is a good idea to start small. Instead of an after school job, let him start with a weekly volunteer job or a job doing chores for a neighbor. Let him learn about himself and what he is capable of. If he wants to express himself by picking out his own clothes, let him do so as much as possible. You might want to give some advice, such as, "You know, most kids your age don't really wear Kermit the Frog T-shirts. Some people might give you a hard time about it." But let him make decisions on his own, when you can.

On the other hand, if your child asks for, or clearly needs, your help with some things, help him. while also teaching him to be independent. If he hates ordering his own food in a restaurant (I do... there is something stressful about having to spontaneously talk to a stranger) you could start by ordering his food for him but having him order his drink or dessert. Role play at home, and give him plenty of chances to try on his own. It can help to suggest he write down what he is going to order, in the way he will say it. "I'd like a medium-rare cheeseburger with tomatoes and no pickles, please." Feeling safe and supported will help kids gain the confidence to try things on their own. The main idea is to encourage independence, while still being there to help if they truly need it.

The biggest thing I can tell you, in the end, is to try to love and enjoy your child no matter what. No, he might not be a soccer star like your nephews or the most popular kid in his school like your friend's child. But he will be amazing in other ways... unique ways that you'll have never imagined. You don't want to miss out on what your child can show you!

(Me off in my own world, while I was supposed to be playing soccer)

16

Aspergers In Females

Although for many years I have believed I had Aspergers Syndrome, I only recently got an official diagnosis. I went for an evaluation at the free clinic at a university about 10 years ago. The doctor there did not think I could have autism, because I displayed some social skills, was able to tell her I felt strong emotions, and had had an imagination as a child. She diagnosed me with ADHD instead. ADHD is closely related to Aspergers, and it did seem to hit home for me... but something was still missing.

Then I was lucky enough to get the chance to speak with Tania Marshall, a psychologist who is an expert on Aspergers in females. According to her and others who are knowledgeable on the topic, Aspergers "symptoms" can manifest differently in females. For this reason, it is often overlooked, and girls either get diagnosed with a multitude of mental health conditions, or go undiagnosed and spend their lives just

17

thinking they're odd or quirky.

In one of my blog entries, I talked about some common characteristics of females with Aspergers. Lets start with...

APPEARANCE - ① They often have little interest in fashion, and dress for comfort or have their own style. For me, this means lots of soft and stretchy fabrics whenever possible. You know those zip-up hoodies with fleece inside, that are often sold at Wal-Mart or Target? I love those, and live in them in the winter. I will wear dresses and skirts too, especially in the summer, but they <u>always</u> have to be comfortable. I have never, and probably never will, owned high heel shoes or tall boots. You'll find me in Converse sneakers, soft boots, or hiking sandals. Some other females prefer dressing in a "tomboy" style.

② They don't spend much time on their hair... It has to be "wash and wear." Learning to braid my own hair was the only hair style I ever learned, and that was largely because, when braided, my wild curls didn't get tangled and weren't as painful to comb. These days I keep it shoulder-length or shorter, and combing it is the most work I put into it each day.

③ They are youthful in looks, dress, appearance and taste. Many women with Aspergers

⑱

look very young for their age, and their hair and clothing styles, or lack thereof, contribute to that. We also often just have a very young "aura" about us. When I am out with my parents or my aunt and uncle, people often assume I am in my teens!

INTELLECT/EDUCATION/VOCATION — ① They may be thought of as gifted, shy, sensitive. etc, as children. They may also have had problems learning. When I was a kid, I was put in a class for "gifted" kids. I didn't do particularly well. Although I had a high IQ, I could not learn the way most teachers taught, through lectures and note-taking. I was also very shy and sensitive, especially around adults. When I got to know people, I would show my personality more. I still am very much like that.

 ② They may have taught themselves to read, or been hyperlexic as a child. "Hyperlexic" means a precocious ability to read words, before starting school, and an intense fascination with letters and numbers. I've seen some articles that refer to hyperlexia as its own seperate form of autism. Anyway, I learned to read when I was about 2 years old, mostly using a board with magnetic letters that my parents would play with, with me. As a kid, I read anything I could get my hands on. I would often get my reading material taken away from me because it was age-inappropriate (such as adult romance novels and articles about sex) since I'd just pick up any book or magazine I could find and start reading. I'd also read at times when I wasn't supposed to, such as in the middle of school lessons. I'd even sneak into the classroom bathroom to read!

③ Highly intelligent, yet sometimes may be slow to comprehend things due to sensory and cognitive processing issues. It may take us longer to respond to questions or to solve problems, only because our differently-wired brains have to translate the information we are receiving. This is a huge problem for me during job interviews. Interviewers expect quick, smart responses. If I could do interviews by writing out my answers, I would knock their socks off! Instead, I often seem confused and tongue-tied.

EMOTIONAL/PHYSICAL- ①They may be emotionally immature and sensitive, moody, prone to depression, prone to temper tantrums or "melt downs," and even to temporary mutism. Sometimes, especially when I am tired or overwhelmed, my emotions are very hard to control. I cannot keep myself from bawling, if I need to. I have gotten good at bawling silently into my sleeve. Sometimes the things that push me over the proverbial edge are seemingly small issues. For instance, once while riding home from vacation with my parents, I was expecting to stop for dinner along the way. My parents had told me we would. To me, it would be the final event in our vacation, and I was looking forward to it. (Keep in mind, I was in my late 20's at the time!) I was pretty much measuring time, and the outcome of the entire night, on the fact that we'd be stopping for dinner. Unbeknownst to me, my parents had quietly discussed it, decided they weren't hungry, and agreed to just ~~s~~ continue driving. Meanwhile, I was still expecting to stop at any moment. When I realized we were in Illinois, I asked my parents when we'd be stopping for dinner, and they said, "We're not." I then had a total meltdown, because I was so angry, frustrated, and sad. My world had been shaken. It was midnight by then, and I wasn't even particularly hungry, but I needed us to stop for dinner! My parents ended up stopping at an A&W inside a truck stop, so I could get a hot dog. But that wasn't the point. I wanted us all to go somewhere together and eat, because that was what I'd been expecting. The whole thing could have easily been prevented by someone saying, "Angel, do you mind if we don't stop for dinner, and just drive straight home? It would have given me the chance to change the plan in my brain and adjust to a new plan.

21

② They stim to soothe themselves when upset or agitated, and also when happy. I stim a lot. You may see me rocking, doing the sign language alphabet with my hands, licking my lips until they were chapped, rubbing my eyes, humming, singing, jumping, etc.

SOCIAL/RELATIONSHIPS- ① They may be very outspoken at times, and get fired up about their passions and special interests. The best way to get me talking is to mention pets, or animals in general. I can also get fired up about certain social justice issues, when I perceive that a group (of people OR animals) is getting screwed over by others. Children in foster care are one of the groups I feel concerned about, and I can go on forever about the things I think are wrong with the foster care system!

② They don't have many "girlfriends," and don't enjoy doing typical activities such as shopping or sitting around talking. It may even be harder in adulthood than in childhood for a female with Aspergers to make friends! I've ~~my~~ tried to join Meetup groups for women, but my problem is that I like to do stuff. I enjoy shopping sometimes if it is for fun things like ~~souvenirs~~ souvenirs, or even for clothes in certain stores for brief amounts of time. I prefer actual activities, such as doing arts and crafts, swimming, bowling, going on rides at amusement parks, hiking, or taking care of animals or children.

③ They often prefer the company of animals. I love all animals! I feel an instant affection and understanding from animals, that I don't often get from humans. Petting a dog or cat, or having one sit on me, can often calm me down when I am feeling anxious, overwhelmed or upset. My dog knows this, and will run straight over to me for a hug when she senses me getting upset. I recently started equine therapy, which has helped me more than any other type of therapy ever has. I would recommend it to anyone!

This list is not exhaustive. It is just a beginning. But you can probably see how the description of a female with Aspergers is much different from the stereotype of an ~~un~~ unemotional, calculating person with autism.

My Answers to Things People Say About ADHD!

For a lot of people, the things they know about ADHD come from TV shows, online memes, and myths. Here are my answers to some things people often say to me about ADHD, as well as to what others have told me people say to them.

① I don't believe in ADHD!

ADHD is not a religion or a moral code. It is a neurological condition! Saying "I don't believe in ADHD" is like saying, "I don't believe in asthma." I know there are some religions that actually don't believe that _any_ illness is real. If you believe that, then "I don't believe in ADHD" is a fair thing to say. But generally speaking, we should think of ADHD (and autism, learning disorders, mental health conditions, etc) the same way we think of other health conditions. It is real, and it effects people every day of their lives.

② You (or your child) can't have ADHD, because you (or your child) are not hyperactive.

First, there are different types of ADHD. If someone has the inattentive type, their bodies may not appear "hyperactive," but their minds are very active!

Second of all, what you see right now is not necessarily how things always are. Many adults and kids with ADHD work very hard to manage their symptoms. They may be using medication, behavior management, exercise, yoga, etc. Back to the asthma analogy... if a person's asthma is being well-controlled with medication, that doesn't mean they don't have asthma any more!

Third, just as with asthma, people with ADHD can have good and bad days. I know that sometimes I go a whole day, or a few days, really being "on top of things." Other days, it is surprising that I manage to get my shoes tied! However you see me today, that may not be how my life is _every_ day.

③ These days, _everyone_ has ADHD!
   It may seem like it. About 2% to 4% of adults and 8% of children are diagnosed with ADHD. So if you know 100 people, 4 of the adults and 8 of the children may have ADHD. But not everyone!

which 4 of these are not like the others???

④ ADHD is just an excuse used by weak or lazy people who don't want to try as hard as the rest of us.

For people who truly have ADHD, it is not an excuse, but an explanation. People who know they have ADHD often put double effort into completing the things that come easily to others.

⑤ If you (or your child) can spend 5 hours doing something you enjoy, then why can't you focus that hard on less pleasant, but more necessary, tasks? ADHD is not really an inability to pay attention, but an inability to control what you pay attention to. Most people who don't have ADHD are able to focus on a less desirable task long enough to get it done, and then go on to spend time doing something they like, for a regulated amount of time. You may tell yourself, "After I finish cleaning the house, I will relax and read a book for one hour." For a person with ADHD, their minds can be glued to something interesting... but if we find something boring, we cannot, for the life of us, focus on it. That is why there are children with ADHD who can spend 8 hours playing video games or working on a science project or doing whatever it is they love... but collapse in a sobbing heap of frustration when asked to do half an hour of homework.

(Helpful hint- If you or someone you know has ADHD)

instead of trying to reward yourself or them ~~after~~ ~~they~~ struggling through an unpleasant task, try incorporating something you love into the task. If your child loves video games but hates reading, instead of saying, "You can play a game after you finish reading for twenty minutes," look for video games that focus on reading skills in a fun way, or find books based on video games. To help him practice writing, ask him to write a guide about how to get through a level of his favorite video game. If you love arts and crafts but hate organizing, turn decluttering your home into a mission to find items you can use in your craft projects, or items to sell for extra money to buy craft supplies. The secret is to find a way to turn on that "hyperfocus" button in our brains!)

⑥ You (or your child) would not have ADHD if you just... (ate less sugar, drank less caffeine, got more exercise, took vitamins, got more discipline, etc.)

There are many different possibilities for helping to manage ADHD. You're right, each of these things you've mentioned can effect some people to some extent. But none of these things, or even medication, can make ADHD go away completely. And while some of these strategies may make a huge difference to some people, they may not help other people at all.

㉗

⑦ I don't think it is fair that people with ADHD get special privileges, like extra time on tests.

Life is not fair! But these "privileges" <u>are</u> fair because they allow people with ADHD (and other conditions that effect learning) to be better able to do the things that others can do without accomodations.

To use our asthma example, imagine a child who gets to skip gym class when his asthma is acting up, or who gets to take a break from the mile run to use his inhaler. Would it make sense to allow <u>everyone</u> to skip gym class, or to pass out inhalers to all of the runners during the Mile Run?

Or how about the child who gets to go to the nurse's office in the middle of each morning, to have her blood sugar tested and to have a snack. Would it be a good idea to test all of the children's blood each morning? Or would it be more "fair" to tell the child with diabetes that she cannot go to the nurses office, and that she'll just have to practice keeping her blood sugar level in check on her own?

To sum up a lengthy explanation, "fair" does not always mean treating everyone exactly the same way. It means making sure that everyone gets what they <u>need</u>.

If you have ADHD, the next time someone makes one of these comments to you, you can hand them this chapter to read!

BULLYING

"Sticks and stones may break my bones, but words will never hurt me." Did you used to say that when you were a kid? I did. It was like a sort of a nursery rhyme. That, and, "I'm rubber, you're glue. Whatever you say bounces off of me and sticks to you!"

But anyone who has ever been bullied knows that these childhood chants are far from the truth. There is an old stereotype of a schoolyard bully who threatens younger or smaller kids and steals their lunch money. The image may accompany a story about a little boy who stands up to a bully, and comes home with bumps, bruises, and the understanding that the "big bully" won't pick on him anymore. However, these days, most bullying is non-physical. It occurs with words... words that do hurt. And instead of one mean kid who picks on everyone, it is often a whole bunch of kids... even a whole grade or a whole school of kids... who gain up against a few targeted victims.

Kids with ADHD, autism spectrum disorders, learning disabilities, and other special needs... especially "invisible" special needs that cause kids who appear like everyone else but act differently... are often the ones singled out by others.

Until I was in the fourth grade, I managed to blend in pretty well. I didn't have a lot in common with them... I didn't care at all about fashion or music videos, I still preferred the sand box over the soccer field, I almost always had my nose in a book, and I refused to get my ears pierced. I was a little louder and more intense than some of the other kids, yet I was also more anxious and easily overwhelmed than they were. I had only one real friend, the only other girl in my grade who would play Little House On the Prairie with me at lunch hour. But there was nobody at my school who teased me. They didn't have to like me, but they accepted me the way I was.

In fifth grade, kids started noticing the difference. The district rezoned the school boundaries, so a lot of the kids I'd grown up with moved to the new school, and a lot of random new kids came to my school. The new kids made fun of me mercilessly! They'd gather around me at recess and make fun of my curly hair, my clothes, and whatever else caught their attention.

The worst thing was, I'd been excited about the new kids at the school! I'd been happy about the idea of making lots of new friends! It had never occurred to me that anyone... let alone <u>all</u> of them... would be mean to me.

At first I took it all in stride. I fought back against the kids who teased me. I would roll my eyes and make snappy comebacks like, "I know you are, but what am I?" and "That's so funny, I forgot to laugh!" (Yeah, it was the 90's, okay?)

And whenever one of them showed me the slightest bit of kindness... if they smiled at me, or said something to me that wasn't an insult... I'd think they were going to be my new best friend. Once, on a field trip, I was standing by myself when a girl said, "Come on, Angel, hang out with us!" She then turned to her friend and confided, "I just feel so sorry for her!" I went home, thrilled, and told my mom that the girl and I were friends now.

Another time, one of the boys in my class did something goofy, and another girl and I exchanged glances and giggled. Deciding we were now bonding, I blurted out, "Hey, Katie, my mom says maybe you can come to my house for a sleepover!" Not too smooth, for a fifth grader. Of course the sleepover (and the friendship) never happened.

By the next school year, I had changed. I had stopped trying. When it was time to do a group project in class, I no longer beamed hopefully at the other kids, but instead stared at my desk until the

㉛

teacher assigned me to be in a group. At lunch time I sat at a table by myself, and on the school bus on field trips I sat with the teacher.

In junior high, the bullying took a turn for the worse. The boys would throw wads of paper and small objects into my curly hair. (It was so frizzy, things would get stuck in there!) The girls were actually vicious. I remember them spraying me with deodorant in the locker room, kicking my ankles in gym class, whispering to me that I was ugly and looked like a boy, and nicknaming me "Hairy" because of my crazy hair. And that is just the things I haven't blocked from my memory.

At night, I would cry because I didn't want to go to school the next day. I would actually pray to God for something horrible to happen to the meanest girls, the ringleaders, so that they wouldn't be at school any more. In the mornings, I was plagued with stomachaches and headaches.

I especially remember being so **angry**. I was angry at the other kids for tormenting me. But I was also angry at the adults in my life for letting it happen. My parents, and a lot of my teachers, knew what was going on. They knew I was miserable. Yet they did not intervene. They let me deal with it alone. And <u>alone</u> was the key word, because that was how I felt, <u>all</u> of the time.

Fast forward twenty years. Now schools hang "Bully Free Zone" signs on the classroom doors, teachers attend workshops on preventing bullying, and there are even laws meant to protect kids from bullies. So, luckily, no kid has to go through what I did, right?

I wish.

In February of 2013, I read a story on Facebook about a 13-year-old boy who had been getting bullied in school. He posted a message on Instagram, saying that he planned to kill himself on his birthday. His mother found out about the message, and immediately took him to the hospital. He was diagnosed with depression.

The boy's mother had known her son was being bullied, but hadn't realized how much damage it was doing to him. Now she posted a message on Facebook, asking her own friends and family members to send encouraging cards and letters to the boy. She wanted him to see how many people loved and supported him.

The plea got passed along on Facebook, and thousands of people from across the world sent letters of support to the boy. Many shared their own stories of surviving bullying. The story even spread to the media, serving to educate others on how dangerous bullying can be.

Anyone would have expected this story to have a happy ending. But when the boy returned to school several weeks later, the same kids began bullying him again. They were now egged on by their own parents, who were angry that the kids had been "falsely accused" of bullying. The irony of encouraging kids to bully someone in retaliation for being accused of bullying was apparently lost on these parents. (The boy ended up being hospitalized again, and eventually switched schools.)

Shortly thereafter I heard a similar story of a 10-year-old boy who was bullied. One day his mother came outside and found him in a tree, with a rope around his neck, ready to jump and hang himself. And we've all heard the stories of kids who have been "successful" at ending their lives, because they were bullied. Some especially cruel bullies even tell their victims, "You should just kill yourself!"

I don't mean to upset readers, but then again, maybe we need to get upset. Some people seem to think that bullying is a normal part of childhood, or even that bullied kids deserve it for being "weak." We need to realize that these kids are being taunted, humiliated, and ostracized on a daily basis. Their spirits are being broken.

I find it shocking that we, as adults, can't stop this from happening. How can we allow children to behave like they're in <u>Lord Of the Flies</u>? I even recently heard a mother saying that her child was being bullied in his preschool class, and that the teacher could not stop it!

In the next chapter I will talk about my ideas for what parents, teachers and others can do in response to bullying. The important thing is to do <u>something</u>! Don't make kids handle it all alone!

Sticks and stones can break my bones...

But <u>words</u> can break my <u>heart</u>!

Responding to BULLYING

① **Give your child alternative places to find support.**
If school is a child's only chance to make friends and have a sense of community, and he's not getting it there, he's more likely to be seriously effected by bullying. So help your child get involved in other places. His talents and interests can lead the way. If your child loves art, sign him up for ongoing art classes with the park district or art center. Enroll him in a club at the YMCA, help him join a sports team, sign him up for a book group at the library, etc. Church can be another great place to get involved. Give him other places to make friends outside of school. In-school activities CAN work, IF bullying does not take place at those activities. For instance, an after-school club at school can be a chance for your child to form friendships with classmates who share his interests. Those friendships might then extend to the school day. But if your child is getting bullied IN afterschool activities, that defeats the purpose! If your child knows he has friends and can have fun after school, it can help him cope with what goes on at school.

② **Be open to what your child has to say. Be his listening ear.** Sometimes parents feel so emotional about their child being bullied, that the child may want to protect them by pretending things are better than they really are. Or, parents will give the child a lot of advice, and the child may think he's going to disappoint the parent if he doesn't handle the situation well enough. Try to be a nonjudgemental listener.

You can ask open-ended questions such as, "What was the best/worst thing that happened at school today?" to try to discern how bad the bullying is. If your child seems to have good experiences at school for the most part, you can focus on helping your child ignore the bullies or find other ways of dealing with them. If it seems like your child is very overwhelmed by the bullying, you will need to get more involved.

③ <u>Ask your child how he would like you to help.</u> This can be another indicator of how serious the bullying is. If your child seems to be more annoyed by it and says there is nothing he wants you to do, it may be just a minor problem. If he's crying and begging you to keep him home from school, you'll know he needs more help and that the bullying is more serious.

④ <u>Involve the school.</u> The teachers and principal should know what is going on, and they should be willing and able to support your child. The teachers can be proactive by trying to identify classmates who

㊲

can be potential friends or allies, and arrange for your child to work with them during group assignments and projects. Giving a few kids, including your child, a special job to work on — for instance, having them work on putting new decorations up on the classroom walls... during lunch hour while the main bullies aren't around, can be a good way to help a student make friends. The teachers and principal should also be prepared to give consequences to the kids who are doing the bullying.

5.) <u>Do not confront the bullies or their parents directly.</u>
In many cases, bullies learn their behavior from their parents. Calling up the parents to let them know what their kid is doing may not have the results you want. At worst, the parents might argue with you or even be verbally abusive... or they might become abusive towards their child, and that could just fan the flames of the bullying.

A better idea would be to ask the school to set up a meeting between you, and the bullies' parents, at school and with the principal's support. If that happens, try not to go into it with an accusing attitude. Instead, plan to calmly and objectively talk about the problem and work towards a solution. If the parents are cooperative, a lot of good can come from such a meeting. If not... at least you know what you're up against!

⑥ Some sources will tell you to document all of the bullying, photograph the injuries, etc. I DISAGREE.

If the bullying has gotten so bad that your child is being injured, and multiple incidents are continuing to happen, without intervention from the school, then I say it is time to get your child out of there. Find another school, or another way to educate your child.

Yes, it may be difficult to get your child into a new school, especially if you can't afford private school or if your child's special needs might not be met at another school in your area. But if there is a will, there is a way. Homeschooling or "unschooling" could be good alternatives if nothing else can be found, or even as a first choice solution. (Some kids do much better when the pressures of the social world are separated from academic learning. They still have plenty of opportunities to make friends and learn social skills, but don't have to concentrate on these things will also trying to focus on math, reading, etc.) I have heard of families who, frustrated by their child's school's lack of response to bullying, pulled their child out of school and ended up convincing the school district to move the child to a different school in the district.

The thing is, if your child is miserable at school, and you are not getting closer to a solution, it is not fair to keep sending them there. Bullying is a form of abuse, and kids need to be protected from it.

(7) <u>Give your child some form of control over the situation.</u> I should have maybe put this one first, since I think it is very important.

Being bullied can make a kid feel very out-of-control, just like any victims of a crime. Imagine you had to go to work every day to a place where almost all of your co-workers taunted you, jeered at you, played pranks on you, and ostracized you. There might be multiple ways you could handle the situation. Maybe you would go to your boss and complain. Maybe you would decide to just ignore it and deal with it, because you know you have good friends outside of work and you don't really care for your co-workers at all anyways. Maybe you'd find a way to rearrange your work schedule to minimize your contact with the problematic co-workers. Maybe you'd quit your job. Maybe you'd even file some sort of harassment charges!

Now imagine that you were not allowed to decide what you would do. Your spouse, or your family members, would decide how to handle it. They might talk to your boss, and then tell you, "We've all decided that you should just keep going to work, and ignore your co-workers. It is good for you to get used to dealing with people like this." And that was that.

You're expected to live with whatever choice your family made for you. How would you feel? What would it be like to not have any control at all?

Try to allow your child to make some decisions about what to do. Does she feel like it is important to her to stay in her school? Does she have some allies in her class who help her deal with being bullied? What ideas does she have that might help the situation?

⑧ Consider letting your child go into counseling or therapy. Studies have shown that kids who are bullied often show signs of Post Traumatic Stress Disorder, even into adulthood. Counseling can give a child a healthy outlet to deal with painful memories and experiences. If sitting in an office talking about feelings is not your child's thing, try art, music, or equine therapy. Signing your child up for a mentor (such as Big Brothers/Big Sisters) is also a helpful option; it can give them a positive role model, who is not a teacher or parent but more of a friend, to help them deal with things.

Your kid's well-being is the important thing! He needs your help to deal with bullying! Please don't leave kids to "handle" it on their own.

What NOT to Say to Someone With ADHD, autism, learning disabilities, mental health conditions, etc (or people whose kids have one of these)

Someone once asked me what they should avoid saying to someone who had ADHD, if they wanted to avoid offending the person or hurting their feelings.

The worst thing I have had someone say, was actually a post on the person's Facebook. They posted as their status, "I think ADHD, autism, depression, anxiety, etc, are just excuses made by weak and lazy people who don't want to work as hard as the rest of us."

Truth be told, I do not put a lot of value into that individual's opinion. He was one of the awful kids who used to bully me in junior high. When he sent me a friend request a few years ago, I accepted. It was my way of forgiving him and putting the past behind me. But from his posts, it seems like he still is as angry as he was when we were 12.

But, back to about his Facebook post. People

with the conditions he mentioned in his post, are anything but weak. I would argue that they are actually super-strong, from having to fight an ongoing battle every day, just to get regular stuff accomplished. A child who spends the day in school, or an adult who spends the day at work or running a household is often exhausted from having to hold themselves together. If you would like an idea of what they go through, think about a language that you are only slightly familiar with, or a profession you know just a little about. Now imagine that you had to spend your work day communicating only in that unfamiliar language, or being expected to perform work at the unfamiliar job as if you've been doing it all your life. Would you be able to do it day after day? You might point out that it would be hard at first but get better as time went on. However, for people with these challenges, it never changes much... especially if they never get any accomodations or learn any coping strategies! They spend their entire lives in a world that remains foreign.

I am not asking you to feel sorry for anyone. We do not want pity, or to be seen as incredibly different and special. We just ask that others understand that we are doing our best. We are trying. We are _not_ lazy or weak!

43

The same can be said for parents whose children have these conditions. You may see a parent in a grocery store, with a 10-year-old child who is having a tantrum on the floor in Aisle 6, screaming and kicking, all because the store is out of Rice Krispies. You might think, "What a spoiled brat! That parent needs to discipline him!"

But it just may be that this is a child with autism who has very strong sensory processing challenges. He may have a very strong aversion to tastes and textures, and Rice Krispies may be one of the few foods he can deal with that doesn't cause him to gag. And when he sees that the store is out of him, to him this means that he will have to eat horrid, disgusting things. A different brand of Rice Krispies won't work, because the box looks different, and the child can detect miniscule differences in the tastes. And in his mind, in what he knows about the world, this grocery store is THE place to buy Rice Krispies.

So he panics. He screams. He is too upset to hear his mother explaining that they can pick some Rice Krispies up at Walgreens on the way home. His world has been shaken. And although he is too distraught to see you there, frowning at him... his mother notices. And feels horrid.

So, what shouldn't you say to someone who is neurologically different from you? Well, I don't have a specific list of phrases to avoid. All I can say is, have empathy. Realize that most people do the best they can, at any given moment or in any situation.

Instead, just offer a smile, or encouragement, or a helping hand. Or, if you can't, then just follow the Golden Rule... If you can't say something nice, don't say anything at all!

45

WHY BOTHER GETTING DIAGNOSED?

Shortly before I was officially diagnosed with Aspergers, I broke the news to my dad that I had an appointment for an evaluation.

My dad has never been enthusiastic about the idea of my having any type of special need... be it depression or anxiety, ADHD, autism, or whatever. He likes to believe that I am no different from anyone else, and that any problems I have are just a result of my being lazy, or wanting attention.

Maybe it is because we have so much in common. Neither of us are particularly social. My dad has a few friends that he's known from childhood. He sees one of them about once a month, and the others less often. I don't even have friends from childhood, and my attempts at making friends as an adult have been clumsy and fruitless. We both have quirky, strong interests, and prefer to spend many solitary hours working on them. Once in a while our special interests will intersect. I remember one time we both became obsessed with a particular movie and watched it together over and over,... about 20 times over one long weekend when my mom was out of town! Neither one of us has any real sense of fashion, although we have our own definite style preferences... him in White Sox T-shirts, goofy hats, and unusual rings or watches he finds on eBay, and me in tie dyes and overalls. and colorful socks. On special occasions, my mom routinely yells at both of us, "You're not wearing 'THAT!'" and sends us back to our rooms to change into outfits she has pre-approved.

You may be guessing that my dad also has Aspergers, or at least ADHD! It could be. He also has the same trouble as I do, following conversations about subjects that aren't on his list of special interests. We have the same odd sense of humor, (my mom calls it "dry,") that others often don't get. When we are together, we crack each other up. It is like we speak our own "Aspien" language. As far as routines and changes, he has even more trouble than me when they are disrupted. If it were up to him, we would probably never go on a vacation or celebrate a holiday.

However, when my dad was a kid people knew even less about autism than they do now, and probably nothing about ADHD. He came from a turbulent family life, so any problems he had were probably blamed on that. From an early age he self-medicated with alcohol, and spent his adult life trying (somewhat unsuccessfully) to fly under the radar.

I, on the other hand, knew I was different, from around 7 years old. Instead of trying to pretend things were perfect, I spent my life trying to figure out exactly who, or what, I was. I was the child of an alcoholic, the grandchild of a schizophrenic, and I read about those topics extensively. Was I an introvert, a highly sensitive person, an indigo child, or... my favorite possibility... an alien stranded on Earth? All of these hit home a little. But when I began learning about ADHD and Aspergers, it was like looking into a mirror.

So, that evening when I started to tell my dad about my appointment, I was not surprised when my dad was doubtful. He kept asking, "So if they say you have Aspergers, then what? Is there a 'cure?' Some sort of shot you can get?"

The whole thing seemed futile to him. Furthermore, he pointed out, he thought that having an official diagnosis would allow me to use Aspergers as an excuse, to get away with things. He said, "You're still going to have to do stuff. You can't just not put the peanut butter away and then say its because you have Aspergers."

(Actually, I think putting the peanut butter away is more of an ADHD thing... but you know what he meant)

I started to reply to my dad. I don't even remember what I said. He misheard me, though, and thought I said, "I am Lincoln." Which made little or no sense. When I rolled my eyes and repeated myself loudly, he said, "Sorry! I'm hard of hearing, you know!" A combination of genetics and the noise of driving a truck has left him with pretty bad hearing loss.

48

Suddenly I realized the analogy there. "Right. So you are hard of hearing. How would you feel if I told you that you just had to try harder to hear people talking? What if I told you that you have to stop focusing on being hard of hearing, and concentrated on listening, you would be just like everyone else?" I said. "Or that you just want people to think you're hard of hearing so that you can use it as an excuse not to listen?"

He sort of laughed, but didn't argue. So I went on, "See, you went to the doctor and found out you were hard of hearing, so you knew what you were dealing with. You can wear hearing aides to help you hear, and that lets you be more independent. I want to have an evaluation to find out what I'm dealing with, so I can be more independent!"

"Yeah, but I don't like wearing my hearing aides. I'm not even wearing them right now," my dad pointed out. Well, that explained the "Lincoln" thing!

"So what is dumber? Someone who wants to see a doctor to find out more about their disability so they can learn to do more in life? Or someone who just ignores their disability and walk around not hearing what everyone is saying?"

My dad replied, "I'm tired. I'm going to bed."

Maybe he realized I was right, or maybe he just got tired of arguing with me. Either way, I think it is a good analogy for any neurological or psychiatric conditions. I think it makes more sense to find out what is going on, and start learning ways to work around it or work WITH it, rather than just try to pretend nothing is going on, and just keep compensating on your own.

ADHD, autism, mental illness, etc, are not EXCUSES for people to just do whatever they want. They are EXPLANATIONS for why people have extra challenges to cope with. When you begin to learn as much as possible about these conditions and how they effect you, you can start to not only "overcome" them, but discover the special talents and abilities they bring to your life.

As always, whether or not to seek a diagnosis for yourself or your child is your own personal choice, and nobody should pressure you one way or the other. But if you were to ask my advice, I would tell you that learning, understanding and knowing about something about yourself is always a great idea!

To Med, or Not to Med? (That is the question!)

When someone has a medical condition such as diabetes or asthma, the decision about whether to treat it with medication is usually obvious... YES! The only real questions are what type and dosage will be best for the individual.

But when the condition is a neurological or psychiatric one, such as depression, ADHD, or anxiety, people tend to hesitate... whether the treatment is for themselves or their children.

One reason is because, when it comes to the brain, nothing seems to be certain. Medical tests can determine whether a person has, for instance, high blood pressure. Medical tests can also monitor how well the medication is working to treat these conditions. But there are no blood tests or urine tests to diagnose conditions that effect the brain. Diagnosis and treatment is often based on observations and opinions.

Added to that, the brain is such a sensitive organ. Our brain contains everything that makes us who we are. When you take asthma medication, you don't have to wonder if it will change your personality! But it can be scary to think about medications that alter the chemical processes in our brains. Some people experience side effects that make them feel sluggish, anxious, or overly-energetic to the point of mania.

Also, we don't usually consider neurological or psychiatric conditions as potentially hazardous. Yes, it can be a pain to have trouble focusing at work or to be nervous and fearful all the time, but it probably won't kill us. While we might consider the side effects of asthma medication to be a necessary evil we put up with in order to avoid asthma attacks that could kill us, with neurological and psychiatric medications we tend to weigh the pros and cons. Will the potential side effects, and the responsibility of swallowing a pill each day, be worth the benefits it will bring us?

So. Should you medicate yourself or your child? There is no definite answer. The choice is a personal one. I get upset when I hear about people pressuring others to take, or not take, medication. Or, one parent accusing another of child abuse because they do, or don't, medicate their child. To me, asking questions is okay. A person might say to another, "I haven't heard of that type of treatment before. How does it work?" But commenting, "You just give your child that medicine because you're too lazy to discipline him," is not okay with me.

This goes for alternative treatments, too. Some people choose to try things like vitamins, exercise, neurofeedback, diet, etc. Saying, "That is so new-agey. You're crazy to believe that it works!" does not help anyone. Nobody would choose to continue any type of treatment, if they weren't getting some sort of benefit from it!

Back to the question at hand: to med, or not to med? While I can't give you a straight answer, I can give you a few things to think about in order to help make a decision.

First, how are you, or your child, functioning currently, without medication? Does your child enjoy school for the most part, or does he hate it? Many kids dislike school, because they'd rather stay home and play. But if he's crying every day because he doesn't want to go, there may be a problem. Is the work too difficult? Is he getting scolded frequently by the teachers for his behavior? For yourself, do you feel like you are able to do your best at work or at however you spend your days? Are you missing deadlines right and left, getting disciplined for saying inappropriate things? Are you unable to manage keeping your house clean, getting yourself and your kids dressed, and other daily life activities? If you or your child have to struggle through each day, you might want to consider medication. Other options or con-current treatments COULD include a behavior incentive plan, accomodations such as more frequent breaks, a weekly maid service to help you keep on top of your household, different types of therapy, etc.

How is home life for you or your child? If your child's teachers complain that he won't sit still, but your family is just very active and outspoken and you are fine with this, you might simply want to work with your child on monitoring his behavior in different settings and situations. The same is true if you have a calm, quiet family and one very active child... you may have to accept that he is different from you, and work on finding acceptable ways for him to channel his energy. But if it seems like your child is physically unable to control his behavior... if he is able to understand what is expected but he just cannot do it... you might consider medication.

Likewise, if you have a really hard time getting through the day at your job because your high level of energy and your trouble concentrating on your tasks, maybe you should think about finding a job that is better suited to you. But if you love your job, and just can't control your attention or behavior, or if your challenges are also manifesting themselves in other areas of your life, maybe medication could help.

Do you, or your child, have friends? It doesn't matter if your child isn't the most popular kid in his grade, or if you aren't the person with the most work buddies... as long as you have at least one or two good friends, and you're happy. Does it seem like your child is able to enjoy her friends and plays well with them? Or does she complain that nobody wants to play with her, because of specific things she does, such as getting too rough or refusing to play by the rules? Do your friends seem to enjoy spending time with you, or do they complain that you say insensitive things or partake in too dangerous of activities?

Most importantly, are you, or your child, happy with yourselves? If you have a healthy self-esteem, a strong support system, and a life that you find enjoyable and manageable, you may not want to make any large changes. But if your child seems frustrated because he's trying so hard to be different... to be calmer, to get along

56

better with friends, to do better school work, to stay out of trouble at home... and if he feels sad or guilty about his own behavior, medication may be something to consider. For yourself, if you are having trouble keeping up with your responsibilities and your relationships, and you seem unable to make necessary changes on your own, medication might help.

The one time when I feel that medication is definitely necessary is when someone is in danger. If an adult or child is so depressed or anxious that they cannot function and are at risk of suicide, if they are experiencing manic highs or such strong anger that they are putting themselves or others at risk, or if they are experiencing psychosis or hallucinations that are causing them to think about hurting themselves and others, medication should definitely be a part of the person's immediate treatment. Ideally this would happen somewhere where the person can be constantly monitored and kept safe, such as in a hospital. Once the person is stable and no longer in danger, they can decide whether to stay on medication and/or try other forms of treatment.

Remember, the final decision about medication

is your own. You can gather as much information and as many opinions as you want from doctors, teachers, articles, friends, family members, random people on social networking sites, etc. But nobody has the right to pressure you into taking, or putting your child on, medication, or to pressure you into avoiding medication. Educate yourself as much as you can about different treatment possibilities, and then make the decision that you think will work best for you or your child.

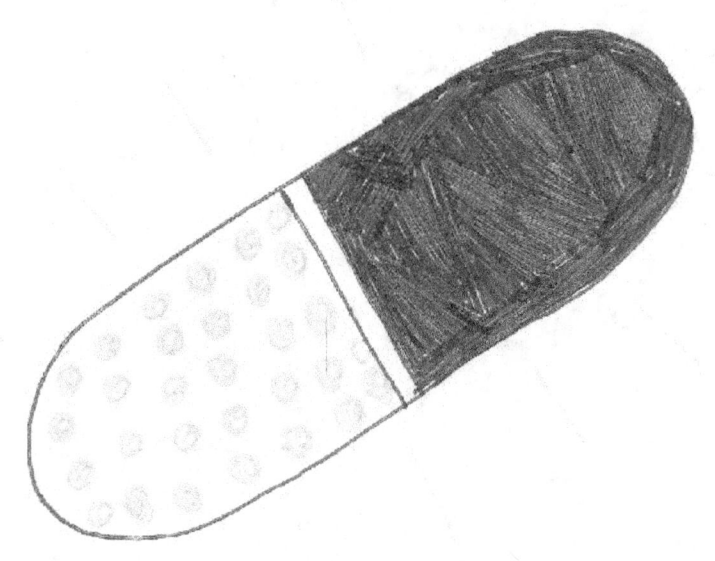

ASK AN ALIEN!

People around the World Wide Web have a lot of questions about ADHD, autism, and neurodiversity. Okay, so they don't actually ask ME these questions. But I thought I'd answer a few anyways! Many of these are about kids, since I am still figuring out the adult stuff myself!

My teenager, who has Aspergers, is very intelligent. However, she has trouble with social skills, and can be immature. I am worried about sending her off to college. She's expressed an interest in going, but I just don't know if she's ready for dorm life!

MY ANSWER- You should talk about this with your daughter, and also an advisor at her school. One option would be for her to start out in community college, so that she could live at home while getting used to the college routine. There are many great community colleges, and many students choose to start out at one... including me! She could get involved in activities if she wants to, and learn to be more independent, while still having the safety of home.

If she is determined to live in a dorm right away, look into 4-year schools within an hour or two of your home. This way, she could come home on weekends when she wants or needs to... and she WILL probably need an occasional break from noisy dorm life!

Most colleges have support programs for students with special needs, and some even have programs just for students on the autism spectrum. An advisor at her high school can probably point you towards colleges with such programs.

In the mean time, if you haven't already, start helping your daughter practice some independent living skills such as doing laundry, managing spending money, etc.

Good luck!

My child was recently diagnosed with ADHD. He is 10 years old. Should I tell him about his diagnosis? I don't want him to feel like he's weird and different from the other kids. I also don't want him to learn to use it as an excuse. But I don't want to lie to him, either!

MY ANSWER - As someone who was not diagnosed with ADHD or Aspergers until adulthood, my point of view might be a little different. I think, if something led you to seek a diagnosis for your child, then you suspected he was a little different from other kids. The chances are, he suspects this too. He may notice when he has more trouble learning than his friends do, gets scolded by the teacher more often, or has trouble keeping friends. When you're a kid, if you notice these things, you automatically think there is something WRONG with you. It can help to understand that it is not his fault, and that ADHD is something he can learn about and control.

One idea is to compare our brains to airplanes and helicopters. Most people are flying airplanes, and your child is flying a helicopter. Airplanes and helicopters are both great. They can both get you where you want to go. But they are different. They have different control panels, and do different things. For most of your son's life, people have been teaching him airplane things, but airplane things just don't work so well for helicopters! Your son will need to learn how his helicopter brain works, in order to get the best performance from it.

My child is 11 years old. She still believes in Santa Claus, the Easter Bunny, the Tooth Fairy, etc. The other kids in her grade do not believe in those types of things. Recently my child got into an argument with some classmates over whether Santa Claus is real. The other kids laughed at her, and she got upset. Should I sit her down and tell her the truth, once and for all?

My ANSWER - I believed in Santa Claus and the Easter Bunny until junior high. Even when others told me it was make-believe, I still insisted on believing.

For me, a big part of it was that I didn't like changes. These fantasy characters, and the routines and rituals that go along with them, are a large part of childhood. Think about Christmas, for example. For many kids, it begins with making a list of the things you want for Christmas. Most kids are taken to the mall to sit on Santa's lap. They have often been doing this since their very first Christmas on Earth. The excitement builds as they start being on their best behavior, since Santa is watching. They may even have an Elf on the Shelf keeping an eye on things. On Christmas Eve, they may track Santa's progress on a website. They may leave out milk and cookies for Santa. They may stay up late in their beds, listening for jingle bells and reindeer hooves. And in the morning... surprise! Santa has been there!

If you take away Santa, you take away all of these rituals as well. Some kids just not be ready to give up these rituals and beliefs.

To me, the important part here is that your child wants to stick up for her beliefs... which is a great quality to have. However, the other kids, in this case, are not wrong. (Except, they should NOT be allowed to make fun of someone!)

What you COULD do is start explaining to your child the concepts of myths and legends. You could bring up mythical beings that your child does not necessarily believe in... maybe fairies, unicorns, or Big Foot. You could explain that it is fun to believe in these things, but that not everyone believes. Explain that believing or not believing are both alright, and that everyone makes up their own mind. Tell your daughter it is best to avoid arguing about these things at school. Explain that Santa, the Easter Bunny, etc, are all mythical beings.

Another idea would be to introduce your child to similar traditions in other cultures. For instance, in Italy children believe in a witch called Befana who comes on the Eve of the Feast of Epiphany and puts candy and presents, or lumps of coal, in children's stockings. In Iceland, for 13 days before January 6, 13 Yule Lads leave treats in children's shoes at night... but for naughty children, they may leave a rotten potato! Many cultures believe in Saint Nicholas or Father Christmas... and in some countries there is also a not-so-friendly helper who scares naughty children.

Different cultural traditions can be fascinating to learn about. You can then present Santa Claus as a fun tradition, and not necessarily real.

Basically, you can help your child to begin accepting that others don't believe in Santa, and that even if she stops believing she can still keep the traditions.

In the mean time, start introducing a few new non-Santa-related traditions that your child can start looking forward to.

I hope that helps!

I just got married. My spouse's brother has High Functioning Autism. He is a young adult. I want to be friendly and spend time with him, but I am not sure how to relate to someone with autism. Any tips?

MY ANSWER- You can read some books or websites about autism to give you an idea of what to expect, but keep in mind that each person, with autism or not, is an individual. Your spouse is probably an expert on his/her brother, and can tell you all about her brother's personality, likes and dislikes, etc.

For many people with autism, new people and situations can cause a lot of uncertainty and anxiety. It can be a good idea to start out getting to know him on his own turf. Find out what he likes to do on the weekends in his spare time, and see if you can join him.

A lot of people with autism may communicate differently or have trouble expressing themselves. It is important to remember that, even if someone does not speak at all, they are a person with feelings and ideas. Avoid treating your brother-in-law like a child. Also, avoid putting him in situations that make him uncomfortable. For instance, if he does not drink, and hates crowds and noise, pressuring him to join you for a guy's night at a bar with your friends is not a good idea. Of course, you could invite him, let him decide if he wants to go, and make sure he has an option of leaving early if he is uncomfortable. Just treat him with respect and kindness, get to know him as an individual, and soon the two of you will be good friends!

My preschooler is diagnosed with autism. He is not verbal, but he is learning to communicate his needs with PECS. He has a tendency to shriek when he gets upset or frustrated, and he has a hard time when he's in an unfamiliar place or out of his routine.

$\longrightarrow$

The problem is my extended family... my parents and siblings, and my in-laws. They do not understand the concept of autism. They think my son does not speak because I spoil him and give him everything he wants. They think I should spank him when he has tantrums, even when I know he's just overwhelmed. My sister has even accused me of having Munchausem Syndrome By Proxy (a disorder in which parents make their own children ill in order to get attention) When we get together for holidays, it is very uncomfortable, and I inevitably end up upset.

MY ANSWER - The problem is, some people choose to NOT learn about new things. They stubbornly stick to the beliefs they grew up with, which may be that childhood disorders are caused by bad parenting.

The first thing you can do is try to educate your family members. I've known of some people who sent a letter out to family members before a family gathering, explaining what autism is and how their child is effected by it. It may include things like, "Please excuse us if I bring Tommy a separate dinner... he has trouble eating new foods and he will feel better if he has something familiar to eat." and positive things such as, "Tommy loves to have people read his dinosaur book to him, and that would be a great way to spend some time with him, if you're interested!"

I also know people who have gone a little further

65

and created blogs or Facebook pages about their child and autism, inviting friends and family members to read them. Or you could send them your favorite book about autism... maybe even THIS book!

Unfortunately, there may be people who still stick to their old opinions about autism. You may have to accept that you cannot change them. You CAN insist that they not speak badly about your child in front of him, or in front of you. You can discuss this with your spouse ahead of time and decide if there is a certain point that you will just leave if things aren't going well. If there are some people in your family who DO understand or want to learn more about autism, you may be able to enjoy your time with them and ignore the others.

Another idea... offer to host some of the family gatherings at your house. Your child may have a better time if he is on his own turf with all of his familiar things around him.

What would be a good gift for a 7-year-old with autism?

MY ANSWER- Since every person is different, it is hard for me to answer this. If the child is able to communicate, you could ask him what kinds of things he would like. Or, you could ask his parents. Many kids with autism have strong special interests, and that can help you get ideas for a gift. If he loves volcanoes, for example,

66

he might like a book or DVD about volcanoes, a puzzle with a picture of a volcano, or a kit that shows him how to make a model volcano.

If you're not going to have a chance to speak with the child or his parents, things that are visually stimulating are often a good pick. Think about things with lights and colors, such as a fiberoptic light, or one of those pictures with sand inside where you can watch the sand moving. A large pillow or stuffed animal can also be great for kids who love soft things and deep pressure!

A single man just moved into the house next door to me. He is quiet and serious, and when I wave "hello" to him he doesn't wave back. Some of the other neighbors have suggested that he might have Aspergers Syndrome. Should I be concerned?

MY ANSWER- If your only "concern" is that this man may have Aspergers, then you probably shouldn't worry. What exactly are you concerned about? Random acts of violence are not a symptom of autism or Aspergers. Some people with autism may react violently out of frustration. For instance, I knew a child with autism who would throw things or pull his mother's hair when he got upset. But if this person in your neighborhood has made it to adulthood and is able to live in a house independently, he's most likely learned safer ways of handling his emotions.

Of course, I'm not saying there is NO chance that this

man could be a danger. Any individual <u>could</u> be capable of violence. Its just that Aspergers is not an indicator of a dangerous person. If you're worried, you could find out your neighbor's name and run a background check on him, and check your state's sex offender database. You should also teach your children not to go into anyone's home or car without checking with you first.

Other than that, just try getting to know your new neighbor! You could send him a friendly greeting card introducing yourself and giving him some tips about the neighborhood.

Many adults with Aspergers (diagnosed or not) are used to people giving them strange looks or making rude comments. Have you ever seen the movie "The Story of Luke?" Its about a young man with autism. Through an organization that helps people with special needs to learn vocational skills, Luke gets a job in an office. On his first day of work one of his new co-workers greets him with, "So you're the newest idiot they sent to help us!" Sadly, that is not so unusual in real life. While many people with Aspergers are uncomfortable around strangers naturally, being treated this way can cause <u>anyone</u> to want to keep to themselves and avoid eye contact.

So my advice is to reach out to your new neighbor and welcome him, and then keep on waving and smiling when you see him. Eventually, he may start waving back!

That is all the sage advice for today. Like I said, I do not have everything figured out for myself yet, which is why I haven't written much offering advice to people who <u>have</u> ADHD or autism. I still have a hard time figuring out how to navigate the world. I am better at giving advice to neurotypical people about how to relate to and treat people like me (with respect and kindness, please!)

I can also say the alphabet backwards, and name all of the states in alphabetical order. But these talents, unfortunately, don't translate very well on paper!

Oh, wise Alien... What is the meaning of life?

I have NO idea!

Neurodiversity
Acceptance!

Many people know that April is Autism Awareness Month. April 2 is Autism Awareness Day. You may have seen people wearing puzzle piece ribbons. Some people also put blue lights on their house in April to "light it up blue for autism."

A lot of people who have autism, and their friends and family members, dislike or have mixed feelings about "autism awareness." They feel that some autism-related organizations focus on autism being a horrible disease that steals the lives of children and families. They focus on trying to find a "cure" for autism.

For people who have autism and can understand and communicate, this can feel like an insult. For us, many of the things that are considered "symptoms" of autism (thinking differently, being sensitive, having trouble relating to others, having special interests and talents, etc) FEEL like large pieces of who we are. When we hear people speak very negatively about autism, it is like hearing, "The world would be better off without you. You'd be better off not existing. I would do anything to avoid having a child who is like you."

I do understand that for some individuals and

families, autism IS very negative. I know children who seem miserable because many ordinary parts of life are painful for them, and because they have no way to communicate what they are thinking and feeling. I have known of people who grew up and had no place to go, because their families could no longer take care of them but they didn't have the skills or support to live independently. I also know of many bright, vibrant people with autism who have dedicated a lot of time and effort into helping others.

Would I like to see autism eliminated? No, I would not like to see myself, my friends and fellow bloggers, and many of the children I've worked with over the years, wiped off the planet.

I WOULD like to see a world where children with autism spectrum disorders don't get bullied or left out by their peers because they are different. A world where people with autism can pursue their favorite interests, and have their abilities and talents appreciated. I would like to take away the idea that people with autism cannot hold jobs, live on their own, or have children. I would replace it with a question: "What does this individual WANT in his life, and what does he NEED in order to make that happen?"

I would like to see every person with autism have

a way to communicate with others... whether it is with their own voices, augmented communication devices, PECS, letter boards, sign language, or any other method that may be devised in the future... and that all of these modes of communication are equally accepted.

I would like to see families get all of the services they need in order to thrive. I would like to see people with autism living their lives to the fullest!

Some people would say all this is too much to hope for, and that it is more realistic to work on just getting rid of autism completely. What do YOU think?

Some people have started calling April "Autism ACCEPTANCE" month. One blogger wrote about how "lighting it up blue" might not be the best symbol for promoting support of a diverse spectrum. She suggested we "turn it on Rainbow" or "Light it up Kaleidoscopic" instead. That made me think about drawing a new symbol that could represent autism in a more positive way... not as something that needs to be cured, but as something that needs to be understood, accepted and appreciated.

But then I started thinking of people I know who have things like Tourette Syndrome, learning disabilities, or Sensory Processing Disorder. I decided I wanted to make something that would represent neurodiversity, or the idea that all of our brains work in different ways.

This is what I came up with.

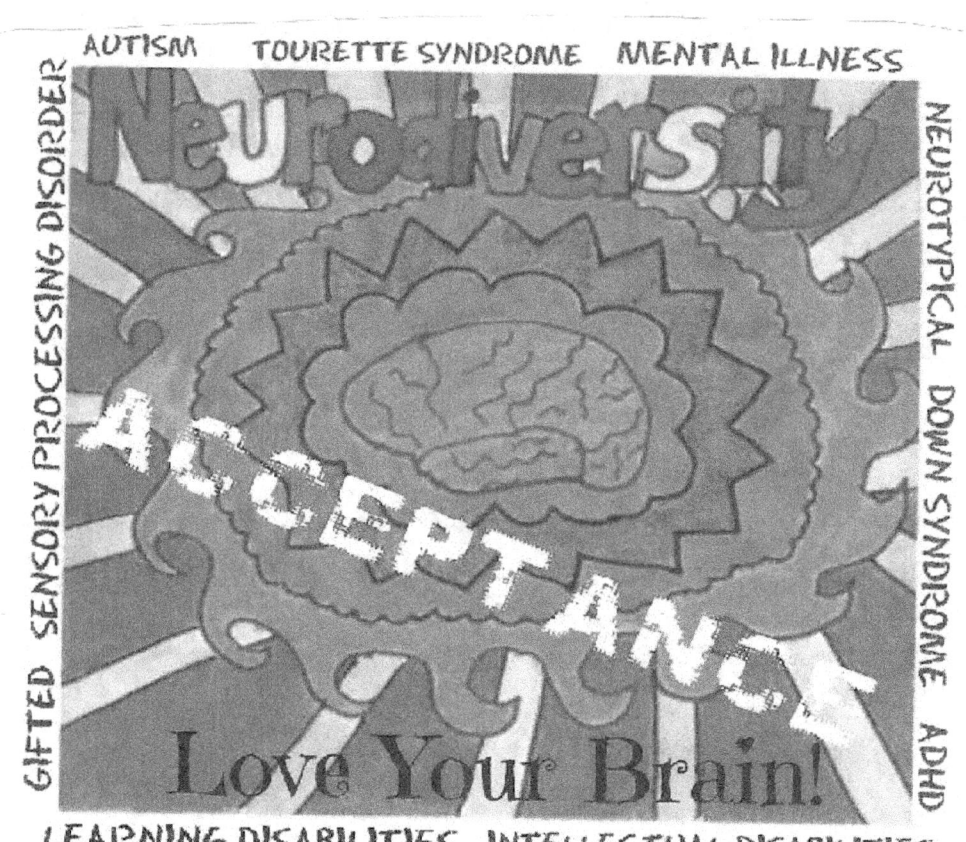

If you like this idea, you can actually buy T-shirts and other products with ~~this~~ this image printed on them, at this website: www.cafepress.com/loveyourbrain.

On, if you have a blog, website, Facebook, Twitter, etc, you can save this image and share it with others. Visit my blog at http://diaryofanallen1.blogspot.com, and you'll find this picture towards the top of

the page. Feel free to add it to your own page or
share it however you'd like! (The only rules are
that you cannot change it and you cannot sell it.)

In the mean time, let's keep dreaming of
a world where we can all belong and be
appreciated!

you may say
I'm a dreamer
but I'm not the only
one...

-John Lennon

MOST IMPORTANT ADVICE

Someone on my blog once asked me what advice I would give to parents about what made me feel bad as a kid, so they could try to avoid those things for their own kids.

The thing that made me feel worst, and still continues to make me feel bad, is when my parents would (and still do sometimes) act embarrassed of me, and tell me to act "normal." My dad didn't notice me that much. But my mom was always telling me to stop talking, stop wiggling, act my age, etc. She would tell me that I looked "retarded" because I would be flapping my arms. She would say things like, "No wonder you don't have any friends!" She would give me a hard look and say, "Chill." Which was supposed to mean that I was being too exhuberant in public. Even my younger brother caught on, and would scold me, "Chill, Angel. Chill."

It was also upsetting when I was seriously anxious or overloaded, and I'd be crying, and my mom would yell at me. She would even tell my brother that I was a brat. I often had that feeling of shame and ugliness.

So try as hard as you can to show your child that you accept and love him the way he is. I know that we can do embarrassing things, and that you feel other people are looking at you disapprovingly. What I would ask you for, what I would have loved from my parents, would be to ignore everyone else, and try to identify WHY your child is doing something. If he is feeling anxious or overwhelmed, you may know of a way to calm him, or you may be able to get him out of the situation. It could be that he is freaking out in the grocery store because it is too noisy and smells too strongly.

On the other hand, he might just be being kind of naughty and trying to get you to buy him a toy or candy. After all, he is still a kid! You should still give consequences if a child is misbehaving in a way that he is capable of doing better. I'm not saying, never give consequences or never tell your child to knock it off. But please be aware of WHY he is doing something and WHY you want him to stop. If possible, don't let the opinions of random strangers unnerve you. Those strangers will probably forget this moment in a few hours. But your child might remember it forever!

Another thing... try not to argue with your spouse (or the child's other parent, whoever it may be) about your child. I would often hear my parents arguing about me, about what they should be doing with me and what was wrong with me. It made me feel horrible. I wanted the earth to swallow me.

If possible, try not to talk about your child while he is in the same house as you... even if he is supposedly asleep. We have sensitive ears, and if <u>we</u> don't hear what you're saying about us, our siblings will repeat it to us with glee. Take a walk, go sit in the car, or even text or email each other, instead of arguing where your kids might hear you.

Emailing may actually be the BEST way to have an argument because you have time to think about what you want to say, and run less risk of blurting out things you don't mean. It also takes the shouting and yelling away, leaving only the words. And the other person can read the message carefully so he can understand exactly what you're saying.

Another thing that is important, especially as kids get older, is knowing when to do things for your child and when to step back. Your child may always need help with some things. But it isn't an "all or nothing" situation. In other words, just because your child still needs a lot of help with certain things, this doesn't mean he is not ready to try other things on his own. And just because he's mastered certain things, that doesn't mean he's ready to face the world completely alone!

It is probably hard to let older kids and young adults be the guides of what they still need. Just do your best. If they feel strongly about wanting to do something independently, and it is relatively safe, let them. Examples of safe risks could be applying for a job you think they'd have a hard time doing, wearing an outfit you think is odd, or trying to befriend someone you think might reject their friendship. Let them try. They might surprise you with their success! And if they don't succeed, remember that making mistakes is a normal part of growing up and being independent. They need these experiences as much as typically developing kids do.

On the other hand, if your child seems to want more help in some areas, be there for them. This could mean helping them write a script for what they should say when ordering pizza over the phone. It could mean allowing your child to do chores for a trusted neighbor once a week, instead of jumping right into a part time job. It could mean letting him take a second semester of driver's ed, instead of getting his license as soon as he turns sixteen.

But to me, the top MOST IMPORTANT advice is just to love your child. Not <u>in spite</u> of who he is, but <u>BECAUSE</u> of who he is.

QUIZ TIME!

Now it's time to find out how much you know and have learned about neurodiversity!

① If somebody is diagnosed with autism, you can automatically assume that...

A. The person feels no emotions or empathy.

B. The person does not want to have friends.

C. The person cannot communicate.

D. All of the above are true.

E. None of the above can be assumed!

② If a person is "stimming" a lot, you should...

A. Let them. It is something they need to do to self-regulate.

B. Explain to the person that they look stupid when they do that, and that they must stop.

C. Punish the person each time that they stim, so that they learn not to do it.

D. Hold the person's hands still to keep them from doing it.

E. Help them find socially-acceptable ways of stimming while they are at school or work.

F. Both C and D are good ideas.

G. Both A and E are good ideas.

→

③ True or false... females with Aspergers always have the same characteristics or "symptoms" as males with Aspergers.

  A - True
  B - False

④ If a person has ADHD, they are always hyperactive. True or false?

  A. True
  B. False

⑤ Most people with ADHD are...

  A. Lazy people who want an excuse not to do things.
  B. Weak people who complain a lot.
  C. Strong people who work hard to maintain their everyday lives.
  D. People who want attention.

⑥ The best cure for ADHD is...

  A. Stimulant medication.
  B. Avoiding sugar and caffeine, and getting regular exercise.
  C. Trick question! There is no cure! However, anything on this list may be useful for MANAGING ADHD.
  D. Behavioral and cognitive therapy.
  E. Neurofeedback.

7 How many people have ADHD?
  A. Everyone
  B. 2-4% of adults and 8% of children.
  C. Nobody... ADHD is not real.
  D. 50% of the population of the USA.

8 If your child is being bullied, you should...
  A. Listen to your child. Find out her feelings, how she has been coping, and what she would like to see happen.
  B. Call the bully's parents immediately and give them a piece of your mind!
  C. Request help from your child's teacher and principal... they should monitor the situation, and keep your child safe.
  D. Tell your child that bullying is just a part of growing up, and that she needs to learn to deal with it on her own.
  E. Tell your child to fight the bullies so that they will be afraid of her and leave her alone.
  F. A and E are both good ideas.

9 The final decision on whether to medicate yourself or your child should be made by...
  A. You, and your child's other parent if it is for a child.
  B. Your doctor (or your child's doctor)
  C. Your boss, or your child's teacher.
  D. A vote by everyone on Facebook.
  E. Your mother-in-law.

82

(10) If your child does not want to play Little League baseball, you should...

   A. Tell him that he needs to, because that is what normal children do.

   B. Tell him that you were a star player when you were in Little League, and that you'll be disappointed if he doesn't play.

   C. Ask him why he doesn't want to play, and listen to his reasons.

   D. Consider letting him choose a different sport or activity that suites him better.

(11.) People on the autism spectrum may have "meltdowns" because...

   A. They want attention.

   B. They are experiencing "sensory overload" from sounds, sights, smells, etc that are overwhelming to them.

   C. They are experiencing strong emotions that they are unsure of how to handle or communicate.

   D. They are trying to ruin everything for you.

(12) The child having a tantrum in the cereal aisle could possibly be...

   A. A child who is used to getting his way all the time.

   B. A child with special needs who is reacting to sensory overload or anxiety.

   C. Possessed by the devil.

   D. Creating a distraction while his mother hides cereal in her purse

   E. Any of the above (except maybe C) could be true.

Now let's see how you did! Here are the answers. Give yourself 1 point for each one you got correct.

1) E ... Nothing can be <u>assumed</u> about a person with autism, because each person is different.

2) G ... Stimming can help a person to stay calm and focus. If a stim is too distracting at school or work, the person could learn to do something more subtle.

3) B ... False! Females with Aspergers often think and act much differently from males.

4) B ... Not everyone with ADHD is experience obvious hyperactivity. Those that do may be able to control it or may not experience it at all times.

5) C ... People with ADHD often work twice as hard to accomplish what others consider everyday activities.

6) C ... There is no definite cure for ADHD. There are, however, many ways of managing it and working with it.

7) B ... 2-4% of adults, and 8% of children, have an ADHD diagnosis.

$\longrightarrow$

8) F... Listening to your child, giving him some control over the situation, and getting the school involved, are good ways of dealing with bullying.

9) A... The choice of whether to use medication is an important, and personal, decision.

10) C or D... Finding out why your child doesn't like the activity will help you decide whether to let him quit or encourage him to continue. It may be a good idea to find an activity that fits the child's personality and needs.

11) B or C... "Meltdowns" are usually caused by being overwhelmed in some way and not having a way to escape or get relief.

12) E... Some of these are more likely than others. The point is, you cannot assume that someone is acting in a certain way because he is "spoiled," or lacks discipline.

★ How many did you get correct?

10-12 = A
7-9 = B
6 or less = Did you even read this book???

The Final Words

I wrote this book because I wanted to help others to understand what it feels like to be me.

Many neurodiverse people "suffer" from their conditions... not because of the conditions themselves, but because of how they are looked at and treated by others.

We are square pegs being jammed into round holes.

I don't mean to say that we should be given special treatment or be taken care of. Most of us want to work, live independently as possible, and contribute to society in some way. Many of us have great gifts to share with the word, if we are allowed to.

→

To me, what I want the most... and I think others do to... is to be understood, and for others to love me FOR who I am, not IN SPITE of who I am.

I hope this book has helped others in some way!

If you want to comment about this book, you can e-mail me at angel-the-alien@aol.com.
← these are underscores

I would love to hear your thoughts!

Until then, goodbye, and thanks for reading.

With love,
from Angel

About the Author

Angel the Alien lives near Chicago, Illinois. Angel loves animals and spends lots of time with her dogs. She enjoys volunteering at an animal rescue organization. Her other hobbies include reading, doing arts and crafts, and blogging. She hopes to become a special education teacher and possibly create her own school for neurologically / diverse children.

You can connect with Angel at her blog, Diary Of An Alien: http://diaryofanalien1.blogspot.com.

www.ingramcontent.com/pod-product-compliance
Lightning Source LLC
Chambersburg PA
CBHW081229280526
45787CB00006B/2587